BHAGAVAD-

GITA

CW01464727

This Book has been published by:

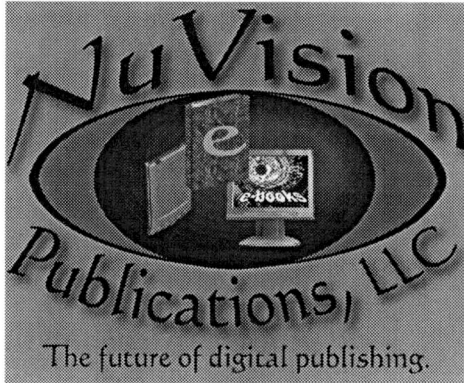

Publishing Date: 2007

ISBN# 1-59547-942-2

Please see our website for several books published for education, research and entertainment.

Specializing in rare, out-of-print books still in demand.

Contact: sales@nuvisionpublications.com

URL: http://www.nuvisionpublications.com

Contents

CHAPTER I

THE DESPONDENCY OF ARJUNA

DHRITARASHTRA:

Tell me, O Sanjaya, what the people of my own party and those of Pandu, who are assembled at Kurukshetra resolved upon war, have been doing.

SANJAYA:

King Duryodhana, having just beheld the army of the Pandus drawn up in battle array, went to his preceptor and spoke these words:

"Behold! O Master, the mighty army of the sons of Pandu drawn up by thy pupil, the clever son of Drupada. In it are warriors with great bows, equal to Bhima and Arjuna in battle, namely, Yuyudhana, and Virata, and Drupada on his great car; Dhrishtaketu, Chekitana, and the valiant king of Kasi, and Purujit, and Kuntibhoja, with Saibya, chief of men; Yudhamanyu the strong, and Uttamauja the brave; the son of Subhadra, and all the sons of Draupadi, too, in their huge chariots. Be acquainted also with the names of those of our party who are the most distinguished. I will mention a few of those who are amongst my generals, by way of example. There is thyself, my Preceptor, and Bhishma, Karna, and Kripa, the conqueror in battle, and Asvatthama, and Vikarna, and the son of Somadatta, with others in vast numbers, who for my service risk their life. They are all of them practiced in the use of arms, armed with divers weapons, and experienced in every mode of fight. This army of ours, which is commanded by Bhishma, is not sufficient, while their forces, led by Bhima, are sufficient. Let all the generals, according to their respective divisions, stand at their posts, and one and all resolve Bhishma to support."

The ancient chief, brother of the grandsire of the Kurus, then, to raise the spirits of the Kuru chief, blew his shell, sounding like the lion's roar; and instantly innumerable shells and other warlike instruments were sounded on all sides, so that the clangor was excessive. At this time Krishna and Arjuna, standing in a splendid chariot drawn by white horses, also sounded their shells, which were of celestial form: the name of the one which Krishna blew was Panchajanya, and that of Arjuna was called Devadatta -- "the gift of the Gods." Bhima, of terrific power, blew his capacious shell, Paundra; and Yudhishthira, the royal son of Kunti, sounded Ananta-Vijaya; Nakula and Sahadeva blew their shells also, the one called Sughosha, the other Manipushpaka. The prince of Kasi, of the mighty bow; Sikhandi, Dhrishtadyumna, Virata, Satyaki, of invincible arm; Drupada and the sons of his royal daughter; Krishna, with the son of Subhadra, and all the other chiefs and nobles, blew also their respective shells, so that their shrill-sounding voices pierced the hearts of the Kurus and re-echoed with a dreadful noise from heaven to earth.

Then Arjuna, whose crest was Hanuman, perceiving that the sons of Dhritarashtra stood ready to begin the fight, and that the flying of arrows had commenced, having raised his bow, addressed these words to Krishna:

ARJUNA:

"I pray thee, Krishna, cause my chariot to be placed between the two armies, that I may behold who are the men that stand ready, anxious to commence the battle; with whom it is I am to fight in this ready field; and who they are that are here assembled to support the evil-minded son of Dhritarashtra in the battle."

SANJAYA:

Krishna being thus addressed by Arjuna, drove the chariot, and, having caused it to halt in the space between the two armies, bade Arjuna cast his eyes towards the ranks of the Kurus, and behold where stood the aged Bhishma, and Drona, with all the chief nobles of their party. Standing there Arjuna surveyed both the armies, and beheld, on either side, grandsires, uncles, cousins, tutors, sons, and brothers, near relations, or bosom friends; and when he had gazed for awhile and beheld all his kith and kin drawn up in battle array, he was moved by extreme pity, and, filled with despondency, he thus in sadness spoke:

ARJUNA:

"Now, O Krishna, that I have beheld my kindred thus standing anxious for the fight, my members fail me, my countenance withereth, the hair standeth on end upon my body, and all my frame trembleth with horror!

8

Even Gandiva, my bow, slips from my hand, and my skin is parched and dried up. I am not able to stand; for my mind, as it were, whirleth round, and I behold on all sides adverse omens. When I shall have destroyed my kindred, shall I longer look for happiness? I wish not for victory, Krishna; I want not pleasure; for what are dominion and the enjoyments of life, or even life itself, when those for whom dominion, pleasure, and enjoyment were to be coveted have abandoned life and fortune, and stand here in the field ready for the battle? Tutors, sons and fathers, grandsires and grandsons, uncles and nephews, cousins, kindred, and friends! Although they would kill me, I wish not to fight them: no, not even for the dominion of the three regions of the universe, much less for this little earth! Having killed the sons of Dhritarashtra, what pleasure, O thou who art prayed to by mortals, can we enjoy? Should we destroy them, tyrants though they are, sin would take refuge with us. It therefore behooveth us not to kill such near relations as these. How, O Krishna, can we be happy hereafter, when we have been the murderers of our race? What if they, whose minds are depraved by the lust of power, see no sin in the extirpation of their race, no crime in the murder of their friends, is that a reason why we should not resolve to turn away from such a crime -- we who abhor the sin of extirpating our own kindred? On the destruction of a tribe the ancient virtue of the tribe and family is lost; with the loss of virtue, vice and impiety overwhelm the whole of a race. From the influence of impiety the females of a family grow vicious; and from women that are become vicious are born the spurious caste called Varna-Sankara. Corruption of caste is a gate of hell, both for these destroyers of a tribe and for those who survive; and their forefathers, being deprived of the ceremonies of cakes and water offered to their manes, sink into the infernal regions. By the crimes of the destroyers of a tribe and by those who cause confusion of caste, the family virtue and the virtue of a whole tribe are forever done away with; and we have read in sacred writ, O Krishna, that a sojourn in hell awaits those mortals whose generation hath lost its virtue. Woe is me! What a great crime are we prepared to commit! Alas! that from the desire for sovereignty and pleasure we stand here ready to slay our own kin! I would rather patiently suffer that the sons of Dhritarashtra, with their weapons in their hands, should come upon me, and, unopposed, kill me unresisting in the field."

SANJAYA:

When Arjuna had ceased to speak, he sat down in the chariot between the two armies; and, having put away his bow and arrows, his heart was overwhelmed with despondency.

CHAPTER II

APPLICATION TO THE SPECULATIVE DOCTRINES

SANJAYA:

Krishna, beholding him thus influenced by compunction, his eyes overflowing with a flood of tears, and his heart oppressed with deep affliction, addressed him in the following words:

KRISHNA:

"Whence, O Arjuna, cometh upon thee this dejection in matters of difficulty, so unworthy of the honorable, and leading neither to heaven nor to glory? It is disgraceful, contrary to duty, and the foundation of dishonor. Yield not thus to unmanliness, for it ill-becometh one like thee. Abandon, O tormenter of thy foes, this despicable weakness of thy heart, and stand up."

ARJUNA:

"How, O slayer of Madhu, shall I with my shafts contend in battle against such as Bhishma and Drona, who of all men are most worthy of my respect? For it were better to beg my bread about the world than be the murderer of my preceptors, to whom such awful reverence is due. Were I to destroy such friends as these, I should partake of possessions, wealth, and pleasures polluted with their blood. Nor can we tell whether it would be better that we should defeat them, or they us. For those drawn up, angrily confronting us -- and after whose death, should they perish by my hand, I would not wish to live -- are the sons and people of Dhritarashtra. As I am of a disposition which is affected by compassion and the fear of doing wrong, I ask thee which is it better to do. Tell me that distinctly! I am thy disciple; wherefore instruct in my duty me who am under thy tuition; for my understanding is confounded by the dictates of my duty, and I see nothing that may assuage the grief which drieth up my faculties, although I were to obtain a kingdom without a rival upon earth, or dominion over the hosts of heaven."

SANJAYA:

Arjuna having thus spoken to Krishna, became silent, saying: "I shall not fight, O Govinda." Krishna, tenderly smiling, addressed these words to the prince thus standing downcast between the two armies:

KRISHNA:

"Thou grievest for those that may not be lamented, whilst thy sentiments are those of the expounders of the letter of the law. Those who are wise in spiritual things grieve neither for the dead nor for the living. I myself never was not, nor thou, nor all the princes of the earth; nor shall we ever hereafter cease to be. As the lord of this mortal frame experienceth therein infancy, youth, and old age, so in future incarnations will it meet the same. One who is confirmed in this belief is not disturbed by anything that may come to pass. The senses, moving toward their appropriate objects, are producers of heat and cold, pleasure and pain, which come and go and are brief and changeable; these do thou endure, O son of Bharata! For the wise man, whom these disturb not and to whom pain and pleasure are the same, is fitted for immortality. There is no existence for that which does not exist, nor is there any non-existence for what exists. By those who see the truth and look into the principles of things, the ultimate characteristic of these both is seen. Learn that He by whom all things were formed is incorruptible, and that no one is able to effect the destruction of IT which is inexhaustible. These finite bodies, which envelop the souls inhabiting them, are said to belong to Him, the eternal, the indestructible, unprovable Spirit, who is in the body: wherefore, O Arjuna, resolve to fight. The man who believeth that it is this Spirit which killeth, and he who thinketh that it may be destroyed, are both alike deceived; for it neither killeth nor is it killed. It is not a thing of which a man may say, 'It hath been, it is about to be, or is to be hereafter'; for it is without birth and meeteth not death; it is ancient, constant, and eternal, and is not slain when this its mortal frame is destroyed. How can the man who believeth that it is incorruptible, eternal, inexhaustible, and without birth, think that it can either kill or cause to be killed? As a man throweth away old garments and putteth on new, even so the dweller in the body, having quitted its old mortal frames, entereth into others which are new. The weapon divideth it not, the fire burneth it not, the water corrupteth it not, the wind drieth it not away; for it is indivisible, inconsumable, incorruptible, and is not to be dried away: it is eternal, universal, permanent, immovable; it is

12

invisible, inconceivable, and unalterable; therefore, knowing it to be thus, thou shouldst not grieve. But whether thou believest it to be of eternal birth and duration, or that it dieth with the body, still thou hast no cause to lament it. Death is certain to all things which are born, and rebirth to all mortals; wherefore it doth not behoove thee to grieve about the inevitable. The antenatal state of beings is unknown; the middle state is evident; and their state after death is not to be discovered. What in this is there to lament? Some regard the indwelling spirit as a wonder, whilst some speak and others hear of it with astonishment; but no one realizes it, although he may have heard it described. This spirit can never be destroyed in the mortal frame which it inhabiteth, hence it is unworthy for thee to be troubled for all these mortals. Cast but thine eyes towards the duties of thy particular tribe, and it will ill become thee to tremble. A soldier of the Kshatriya tribe hath no duty superior to lawful war, and just to thy wish the door of heaven is found open before thee, through this glorious unsought fight which only fortune's favored soldiers may obtain. But if thou wilt not perform the duty of thy calling and fight out the field, thou wilt abandon thy natural duty and thy honor, and be guilty of a crime. Mankind will speak of thy ill fame as infinite, and for one who hath been respected in the world ill fame is worse than death. The generals of the armies will think that thy retirement from the field arose from fear, and even amongst those by whom thou wert wont to be thought great of soul thou shalt become despicable. Thine enemies will speak of thee in words which are unworthy to be spoken, depreciating thy courage and abilities; what can be more dreadful than this! If thou art slain thou shalt attain heaven; if victorious, the world shall be thy reward; wherefore, son of Kunti, arise with determination fixed for the battle. Make pleasure and pain, gain and loss, victory and defeat, the same to thee, and then prepare for battle, for thus and thus alone shalt thou in action still be free from sin.

"Thus before thee has been set the opinion in accordance with the Sankhya doctrine, speculatively; now hear what it is in the practical, devotional one, by means of which, if fully imbued therewith, thou shalt forever burst the bonds of Karma and rise above them. In this system of Yoga no effort is wasted, nor are there any evil consequences, and even a little of this practice delivereth a man from great risk. In this path there is only one single object, and this of a steady, constant nature; but widely-branched is the faith and infinite are the objects of those who follow not this system.

"The unwise, delighting in the controversies of the Vedas, tainted with worldly lusts, and preferring a transient enjoyment of heaven to eternal absorption, whilst they declare there is no other reward, pronounce, for the attainment of worldly riches and enjoyments, flowery sentences which promise rewards in future births for present action, ordaining also many special ceremonies the fruit of which is merit leading to power and objects of enjoyment. But those who thus desire riches and enjoyment have no certainty of soul and least hold on meditation. The subject of the Vedas is the assemblage of the three qualities. Be thou free from these qualities, O Arjuna! Be free from the 'pairs of opposites' and constant in the quality of Sattva, free from worldly anxiety and the desire to preserve present possessions, self-centered and uncontrolled by objects of mind or sense. As many benefits as there are in a tank stretching free on all sides, so many are there for a truth-realizing Brahman in all the Vedic rites.

"Let, then, the motive for action be in the action itself, and not in the event. Do not be incited to actions by the hope of their reward, nor let thy life be spent in inaction. Firmly persisting, in Yoga, perform thy duty, O Dhananijaya, and laying aside all desire for any benefit to thyself from action, make the event equal to thee, whether it be success or failure. Equal-mindedness is called Yoga.

"Yet the performance of works is by far inferior to mental devotion, O despiser of wealth. Seek an asylum, then, in this mental devotion, which is knowledge; for the miserable and unhappy are those whose impulse to action is found in its reward. But he who by means of Yoga is mentally devoted dismisses alike successful and unsuccessful results, being beyond them; Yoga is skill in the performance of actions: therefore do thou aspire to this devotion. For those who are thus united to knowledge and devoted, who have renounced all reward for their actions, meet no rebirth in this life, and go to that eternal blissful abode which is free from all disease and untouched by troubles.

"When thy heart shall have worked through the snares of delusion, then thou wilt attain to high indifference as to those doctrines which are already taught or which arc yet to be taught. When thy mind once liberated from the Vedas shall be fixed immovably in contemplation, then shalt thou attain to devotion."

ARJUNA:

"What, O Kesava, is the description of that wise and devoted man who is fixed in contemplation and confirmed in spiritual knowledge? What may such a sage declare? Where may he dwell? Does he move and act like other men?"

KRISHNA:

"A man is said to be confirmed in spiritual knowledge when he forsaketh every desire which entereth into his heart, and of himself is happy and content in the Self through the Self. His mind is undisturbed in adversity; he is happy and contented in prosperity, and he is a stranger to anxiety, fear, and anger. Such a man is called a Muni. When in every condition he receives each event, whether favorable or unfavorable,with an equal mind which neither likes nor dislikes, his wisdom is established, and, having met good or evil, neither rejoiceth at the one nor is cast down by the other. He is confirmed in spiritual knowledge, when, like the tortoise, he can draw in all his senses and restrain them from their wonted purposes. The hungry man loseth sight of every other object but the gratification of his appetite, and when he is become acquainted with the Supreme, he loseth all taste for objects of whatever kind. The tumultuous senses and organs hurry away by force the heart even of the wise man who striveth after perfection. Let a man, restraining all these, remain in devotion at rest in me, his true self; for he who hath his senses and organs in control possesses spiritual knowledge.

"He who attendeth to the inclinations of the senses, in them hath a concern; from this concern is created passion, from passion anger, from anger is produced delusion, from delusion a loss of the memory, from the loss of memory loss of discrimination, and from loss of discrimination loss of all! But he who, free from attachment or repulsion for objects, experienceth them through the senses and organs, with his heart obedient to his will, attains to tranquillity of thought. And this tranquil state attained, therefrom shall soon result a separation from all troubles; and his mind being thus at ease, fixed upon one object, it embraceth wisdom from all sides. The man whose heart and mind are not at rest is without wisdom or the power of contemplation; who doth not practice reflection, hath no calm; and how can a man without calm obtain happiness? The uncontrolled heart, following the dictates of the moving passions, snatcheth away his spiritual knowledge, as the storm the bark upon the raging ocean. Therefore, O great-armed one, he is possessed of spiritual knowledge whose senses are withheld from objects of sense. What is night to those who are unenlightened is as day to his gaze; what seems as day is known to him as night, the night of ignorance. Such is the self-governed Sage!

"The man whose desires enter his heart, as waters run into the unswelling passive ocean, which, though ever fall, yet does not quit its bed, obtaineth happiness; not he who lusteth in his lusts.

"The man who, having abandoned all desires, acts without covetousness, selfishness, or pride, deeming himself neither actor nor possessor, attains to rest. This, O son of Pritha, is dependence upon the Supreme Spirit, and he who possesseth it goeth no more astray; having obtained it, if therein established at the hour of death, he passeth on to Nirvana in the Supreme."

CHAPTER III

THE RIGHT PERFORMANCE OF ACTION

ARJUNA:

"If according to thy opinion, O giver of all that men ask, knowledge is superior to the practice of deeds, why then dost thou urge me to engage in an undertaking so dreadful as this? Thou, as it were with doubtful speech, confusest my reason; wherefore choose one method amongst them by which I may obtain happiness and explain it unto me."

KRISHNA:

"It hath before been declared by me, O sinless one, that in this world there are two modes of devotion: that of those who follow the Sankhya, or speculative science, which is the exercise of reason in contemplation; and that of the followers of the Yoga school, which is devotion in the performance of action.

"A man enjoyeth not freedom from action from the non-commencement of that which he hath to do; nor doth he obtain happiness from a total abandonment of action. No one ever resteth a moment inactive. Every man is involuntarily urged to act by the qualities which spring from nature. He who remains inert, restraining the senses and organs, yet pondering with his heart upon objects of sense, is called a false pietist of bewildered soul. But he who having subdued all his passions performeth with his active faculties all the duties of life, unconcerned as to their result, is to be esteemed. Do thou perform the proper actions: action is superior to inaction. The journey of thy mortal frame cannot be accomplished by inaction. All actions performed other than as sacrifice unto God make the actor bound by action. Abandon, then, O son of Kunti, all selfish motives, and in action perform thy duty for him alone. When in ancient times the lord of creatures had formed mankind, and at the same time appointed his worship, he spoke and said: 'With this worship, pray for increase, and let it be for you

17

Kamadhuk, the cow of plenty, on which ye shall depend for the accomplishment of all your wishes. With this nourish the Gods, that the Gods may nourish you; thus mutually nourishing ye shall obtain the highest felicity. The Gods being nourished by worship with sacrifice, will grant you the enjoyment of your wishes. He who enjoyeth what hath been given unto him by them, and offereth not a portion unto them, is even as a thief. But those who eat not but what is left of the offerings shall be purified of all their transgressions. Those who dress their meat but for themselves eat the bread of sin, being themselves sin incarnate. Beings are nourished by food, food is produced by rain, rain comes from sacrifice, and sacrifice is performed by action. Know that action comes from the Supreme Spirit who is one; wherefore the all-pervading Spirit is at all times present in the sacrifice.

"He who, sinfully delighting in the gratification of his passions, doth not cause this wheel thus already set in motion to continue revolving, liveth in vain, O son of Pritha.

"But the man who only taketh delight in the Self within, is satisfied with that and content with that alone, hath no selfish interest in action. He hath no interest either in that which is done or that which is not done; and there is not, in all things which have been created, any object on which he may place dependence. Therefore perform thou that which thou hast to do, at all times unmindful of the event; for the man who doeth that which he hath to do, without attachment to the result, obtaineth the Supreme. Even by action Janaka and others attained perfection. Even if the good of mankind only is considered by thee, the performance of thy duty will be plain; for whatever is practiced by the most excellent men, that is also practiced by others. The world follows whatever example they set. There is nothing, O son of Pritha, in the three regions of the universe which it is necessary for me to perform, nor anything possible to obtain which I have not obtained; and yet I am constantly in action. If I were not indefatigable in action, all men would presently follow my example, O son of Pritha. If I did not perform actions these creatures would perish; I should be the cause of confusion of castes, and should have slain all these creatures. O son of Bharata, as the ignorant perform the duties of life from the hope of reward, so the wise man, from the wish to bring the world to duty and benefit mankind, should perform his actions without motives of interest. He should not create confusion in the understandings of the ignorant, who are inclined to outward works, but by being himself engaged in action should cause them to act also. All actions are effected by the qualities of nature. The man deluded by ignorance thinks, 'I am the actor.' But he, O strong-armed one! who is acquainted with the nature of the two distinctions of cause and effect, knowing that the qualities act only in the qualities, and that the Self is distinct from them, is not attached in action.

"Those who have not this knowledge are interested in the actions thus brought about by the qualities; and he who is perfectly enlightened should not unsettle those whose discrimination is weak and knowledge incomplete, nor cause them to relax from their duty.

"Throwing every deed on me, and with thy meditation fixed upon the Higher Self, resolve to fight, without expectation, devoid of egotism and free from anguish.

"Those men who constantly follow this my doctrine without reviling it, and with a firm faith, shall be emancipated even by actions; but they who revile it and do not follow it are bewildered in regard to all knowledge, and perish, being devoid of discrimination.

"But the wise man also seeketh for that which is homogeneous with his own nature. All creatures act according to their natures; what, then, will restraint effect? In every purpose of the senses are fixed affection and dislike. A wise man should not fall in the power of these two passions, for they are the enemies of man. It is better to do one's own duty, even though it be devoid of excellence, than to perform another's duty well. It is better to perish in the performance of one's own duty; the duty of another is full of danger."

ARJUNA:

"By what, O descendant of Vrishni, is man propelled to commit offenses; seemingly against his will and as if constrained by some secret force?"

KRISHNA:

"It is lust which instigates him. It is passion, sprung from the quality of *rajas*; insatiable, and full of sin. Know this to be the enemy of man on earth. As the flame is surrounded by smoke, and a mirror by rust, and as the womb envelops the foetus, so is the universe surrounded by this passion. By this -- the constant enemy of the wise man, formed from desire which rageth like fire and is never to be appeased -- is discriminative knowledge surrounded. Its empire is over the senses and organs, the thinking principle and the discriminating faculty also; by means of these it cloudeth discrimination and deludeth the Lord of the body. Therefore, O best of the descendants of Bharata, at the very outset restraining thy senses, thou shouldst conquer this sin which is the destroyer of knowledge and of spiritual discernment.

"The senses and organs are esteemed great, but the thinking self is greater than they. The discriminating principle is greater than the thinking self, and that which is greater than the discriminating principle is He. Thus knowing what is greater than the discriminating principle

19

and strengthening the lower by the Higher Self, do thou of mighty arms slay this foe which is formed from desire and is difficult to seize."

CHAPTER IV

SPIRITUAL KNOWLEDGE

KRISHNA:

"This exhaustless doctrine of Yoga I formerly taught unto Vivasvat; Vivasvat communicated it to Manu and Manu made it known unto Ikshvaku; and being thus transmitted from one unto another it was studied by the Rajarshis, until at length in the course of time the mighty art was lost, O harasser of thy foes! It is even the same exhaustless, secret, eternal doctrine I have this day communicated unto thee because thou art my devotee and my friend."

ARJUNA:

"Seeing that thy birth is posterior to the life of Ikshvaku, how am I to understand that thou wert in the beginning the teacher of this doctrine?"

KRISHNA:

"Both I and thou have passed through many births, O harasser of thy foes! Mine are known unto me, but thou knowest not of thine.

"Even though myself unborn, of changeless essence, and the lord of all existence, yet in presiding over nature -- which is mine -- I am born but through my own *maya*, the mystic power of self-ideation, the eternal thought in the eternal mind. I produce myself among creatures, O son of Bharata, whenever there is a decline of virtue and an insurrection of vice and injustice in the world; and thus I incarnate from age to age for the preservation of the just, the destruction of the wicked, and the establishment of righteousness. Whoever, O Arjuna, knoweth my divine birth and actions to be even so doth not upon quitting his mortal frame enter into another, for he entereth into me. Many who were free from craving, fear, and anger, filled with my spirit, and who depended upon me, having been purified by the ascetic fire of

21

knowledge, have entered into my being. In whatever way men approach me, in that way do I assist them; but whatever the path taken by mankind, that path is mine, O son of Pritha. Those who wish for success to their works in this life sacrifice to the gods; and in this world success from their actions soon corneth to pass.

"Mankind was created by me of four castes distinct in their principles and in their duties according to the natural distribution of the actions and qualities. Know me, then, although changeless and not acting, to be the author of this. Actions affect me not, nor have I any expectations from the fruits of actions. He who comprehendeth me to be thus is not held by the bonds of action to rebirth. The ancients who longed for eternal salvation, having discovered this, still performed works. Wherefore perform thou works even as they were performed by the ancients in former times.

"Even sages have been deluded as to what is action and what inaction; therefore I shall explain to thee what is action by a knowledge of which thou shalt be liberated from evil. One must learn well what is action to be performed, what is not to be, and what is inaction. The path of action is obscure. That man who sees inaction in action and action in inaction is wise among men; he is a true devotee and a perfect performer of all action.

"Those who have spiritual discrimination call him wise whose undertakings are all free from desire, for his actions are consumed in the fire of knowledge. He abandoneth the desire to see a reward for his actions, is free, contented, and upon nothing dependeth, and although engaged in action he really doeth nothing; he is not solicitous of results, with mind and body subdued and being above enjoyment from objects, doing with the body alone the acts of the body, he does not subject himself to rebirth. He is contented with whatever he receives fortuitously, is free from the influence of the 'pairs of opposites' and from envy, the same in success and failure; even though he act he is not bound by the bonds of action. All the actions of such a man who is free from self-interest, who is devoted, with heart set upon spiritual knowledge, and whose acts are sacrifices for the sake of the Supreme, are dissolved and left without effect on him. The Supreme Spirit is the act of offering, the Supreme Spirit is the sacrificial butter offered in the fire which is the Supreme Spirit, and unto the Supreme Spirit goeth he who maketh the Supreme Spirit the object of his meditation in performing his actions.

"Some devotees give sacrifice to the Gods, while others, lighting the subtler fire of the Supreme Spirit, offer up themselves; still others make sacrifice with the senses, beginning with hearing, in the fire of self-restraint, and some give up all sense-delighting sounds, and others again, illuminated by spiritual knowledge, sacrifice all the functions of the senses and vitality in the fire of devotion through self-constraint. There are also those who perform sacrifice by wealth given in alms, by mortification, by devotion, and by silent study. Some sacrifice the up-breathing in the down-breathing and the down-breathing in the up-breathing by blocking up the channels of inspiration and expiration; and others by stopping the movements of both the life breaths; still others by abstaining from food sacrifice life in their life.

"All these different kinds of worshipers are by their sacrifices purified from their sins; but they who partake of the perfection of spiritual knowledge arising from such sacrifices pass into the eternal Supreme Spirit. But for him who maketh no sacrifices there is no part nor lot in this world; how then shall he share in the other, O best of the Kurus?

"All these sacrifices of so many kinds are displayed in the sight of God; know that they all spring from action, and, comprehending this, thou shalt obtain an eternal release. O harasser of thy foes, the sacrifice through spiritual knowledge is superior to sacrifice made with material things; every action without exception is comprehended in spiritual knowledge, O son of Pritha. Seek this wisdom by doing service, by strong search, by questions, and by humility; the wise who see the truth will communicate it unto thee, and knowing which thou shalt never again fall into error, O son of Bharata. By this knowledge thou shalt see all things and creatures whatsoever in thyself and then in me. Even if thou wert the greatest of all sinners, thou shalt be able to cross over all sins in the bark of spiritual knowledge. As the natural fire, O Arjuna, reduceth fuel to ashes, so does the fire of knowledge reduce all actions to ashes. There is no purifier in this world to be compared to spiritual knowledge; and he who is perfected in devotion findeth spiritual knowledge springing up spontaneously in himself in the progress of time. The man who restraineth the senses and organs and hath faith obtaineth spiritual knowledge, and having obtained it he soon reacheth supreme tranquillity; but the ignorant, those full of doubt and without faith, are lost. The man of doubtful mind hath no happiness either in this world or in the next or in any other. No actions bind that man who through spiritual discrimination hath renounced action and cut asunder all doubt by knowledge, O despiser of wealth. Wherefore, O son of Bharata, having cut asunder with the sword of spiritual knowledge this doubt which existeth in thy heart, engage in the performance of action. Arise!"

CHAPTER V

RENUNCIATION OF ACTION

ARJUNA:

"At one time, O Krishna, thou praisest the renunciation of action, and yet again its right performance. Tell me with certainty which of the two is better."

KRISHNA:

"Renunciation of action and devotion through action are both means of final emancipation, but of these two devotion through action is better than renunciation. He is considered to be an ascetic who seeks nothing and nothing rejects, being free from the influence of the 'pairs of opposites,'O thou of mighty arms; without trouble he is released from the bonds forged by action. Children only and not the wise speak of renunciation of action and of right performance of action as being different. He who perfectly practices the one receives the fruits of both, and the place which is gained by the renouncer of action is also attained by him who is devoted in action. That man seeth with clear sight who seeth that the Sankhya and the Yoga doctrines are identical. But to attain to true renunciation of action without devotion through action is difficult, O thou of mighty arms; while the devotee who is engaged in the right practice of his duties approacheth the Supreme Spirit in no long time. The man of purified heart, having his body fully controlled, his senses restrained, and for whom the only self is the Self of all creatures, is not tainted although performing actions. The devotee who knows the divine truth thinketh 'I am doing nothing' in seeing, hearing, touching, smelling, eating, moving, sleeping, breathing; even when speaking, letting go or taking, opening or closing his eyes, he sayeth, 'the senses and organs move by natural impulse to their appropriate objects.' Whoever in acting dedicates his actions to the Supreme Spirit and puts aside all selfish interest in their result is untouched by sin, even as the leaf of the lotus is unaffected by the waters. The truly devoted, for the purification of the heart, perform actions with their bodies, their minds, their understanding, and their senses, putting away all self-interest. The man who is devoted and not attached to the fruit of his actions obtains tranquillity; whilst he who through desire has attachment for the fruit of action is bound down thereby. The self-restrained sage having with his heart renounced all actions, dwells at rest in the 'nine gate city of his abode,' neither acting nor causing to act.

"The Lord of the world creates neither the faculty of acting, nor actions, nor the connection between action and its fruits; but nature prevaileth in these. The Lord receives no man's deeds, be they sinful or full of merit. The truth is obscured by that which is not true, and therefore all creatures are led astray. But in those for whom knowledge of the true Self has dispersed ignorance, the Supreme, as if lighted by the sun, is revealed. Those whose souls are in the Spirit, whose asylum is in it, who are intent on it and purified by knowledge from all sins, go to that place from which there is no return.

"The illuminated sage regards with equal mind an illuminated, selfless Brahmin, a cow, an elephant, a dog, and even an outcaste who eats the flesh of dogs. Those who thus preserve an equal mind gain heaven even in this life, for the Supreme is free from sin and equal-minded; therefore they rest in the Supreme Spirit. The man who knoweth the Supreme Spirit, who is not deluded, and who is fixed on him, doth not rejoice at obtaining what is pleasant, nor grieve when meeting what is unpleasant. He whose heart is not attached to objects of sense finds pleasure within himself, and, through devotion, united with the Supreme, enjoys imperishable bliss. For those enjoyments which arise through the contact of the senses with external objects are wombs of pain, since they have a beginning and an end; O son of Kunti, the wise man delighteth not in these. He who, while living in this world and before the liberation of the soul from the body, can resist the impulse arising from desire and anger is a devotee and blessed. The man who is happy within himself, who is illuminated within, is a devotee, and partaking of the nature of the Supreme Spirit, he is merged in it. Such illuminated sages whose sins are exhausted, who are free from delusion, who have their senses and organs under control, and devoted to the good of all creatures, obtain assimilation with the Supreme Spirit. Assimilation with the Supreme Spirit is on both sides of death for those who are free from desire and anger, temperate, of thoughts restrained; and who are acquainted with the true Self.

"The anchorite who shutteth his placid soul away from all sense of touch, with gaze fixed between his brows; who maketh the breath to pass through both his nostrils with evenness alike in inspiration and expiration, whose senses and organs together with his heart and understanding are under control, and who hath set his heart upon liberation and is ever free from desire and anger, is emancipated from birth and death even in this life. Knowing that I, the great Lord of all worlds, am the enjoyer of all sacrifices and penances and the friend of all creatures, he shall obtain me and be blessed."

CHAPTER VI

SELF-RESTRAINT

KRISHNA:

"He who, unattached to the fruit of his actions, performeth such actions as should be done is both a renouncer of action and a devotee of right action; not he who liveth without kindling the sacrificial fire and without ceremonies. Know, O son of Pandu, that what they call *Sannyasa* or a forsaking of action is the same as *Yoga* or the practice of devotion. No one without having previously renounced all intentions can be devoted. Action is said to be the means by which the wise man who is desirous of mounting to meditation may reach thereto; so cessation from action is said to be the means for him who hath reached to meditation. When he hath renounced all intentions and is devoid of attachment to action in regard to objects of sense, then he is called one who hath ascended to meditation. He should raise the self by the Self; let him not suffer the Self to be lowered; for Self is the friend of self, and, in like manner, self is its own enemy. Self is the friend of the man who is self-conquered; so self like a foe hath enmity to him who is not self-conquered. The Self of the man who is self-subdued and free from desire and anger is intent on the Supreme Self in heat and cold, in pain and pleasure, in honor and ignominy. The man who hath spiritual knowledge and discernment, who standeth upon the pinnacle, and hath subdued the senses, to whom gold and stone are the same, is said to be devoted. And he is esteemed among all who, whether amongst his friends and companions, in the midst of enemies or those who stand aloof or remain neutral, with those who love and those who hate, and in the company of sinners or the righteous, is of equal mind.

"He who has attained to meditation should constantly strive to stay at rest in the Supreme, remaining in solitude and seclusion, having his body and his thoughts under control, without possessions and free from hope. He should in an undefiled spot place his seat, firm, neither too high nor too low, and made of kusa grass which is covered with a skin

29

and a cloth. There, for the self's purification he should practice meditation with his mind fixed on one point, the modifications of the thinking principle controlled and the action of the senses and organs restrained. Keeping his body, head, and neck firm and erect, with mind determined, and gaze directed to the tip of his nose without looking in any direction, with heart at peace and free from fear, the Yogi should remain, settled in the vow of a Brahmachari, his thoughts controlled, and heart fixed on me. The devotee of controlled mind who thus always bringeth his heart to rest in the Supreme reacheth that tranquillity, the supreme assimilation with me.

"This divine discipline, Arjuna, is not to be attained by the man who eateth more than enough or too little, nor by him who hath a habit of sleeping much, nor by him who is given to over watching. The meditation which destroyeth pain is produced in him who is moderate in eating and in recreation, of moderate exertion in his actions, and regulated in sleeping and waking. When the man, so living, centers his heart in the true Self and is exempt from attachment to all desires, he is said to have attained to yoga. Of the sage of self-centered heart, at rest and free from attachment to desires, the simile is recorded, 'as a lamp which is sheltered from the wind flickereth not.' When regulated by the practice of yoga and at rest, seeing the self by the self, he is contented; when he becometh acquainted with that boundless bliss which is not connected with objects of the senses, and being where he is not moved from the reality; having gained which he considereth no other superior to it, and in which, being fixed, he is not moved even by the greatest grief; know that this disconnection from union with pain is distinguished as yoga, spiritual union or devotion, which is to be striven after by a man with faith and steadfastly.

"When he hath abandoned every desire that ariseth from the imagination and subdued with the mind the senses and organs which impel to action in every direction, being possessed of patience, he by degrees finds rest; and, having fixed his mind at rest in the true Self, he should think of nothing else. To whatsoever object the inconstant mind goeth out he should subdue it, bring it back, and place it upon the Spirit. Supreme bliss surely cometh to the sage whose mind is thus at peace; whose passions and desires are thus subdued; who is thus in the true Self and free from sin. He who is thus devoted and free from sin obtaineth without hindrance the highest bliss -- union with the Supreme Spirit. The man who is endued with this devotion and who seeth the unity of all things perceiveth the Supreme Soul in all things and all things in the Supreme Soul. He who seeth me in all things and all things in me looseneth not his hold on me and I forsake him not. And whosoever, believing in spiritual unity, worshipeth me who am in all things, dwelleth with me in whatsoever condition he may be. He, O Arjuna, who by the similitude found in himself seeth but one essence in all things, whether they be evil or good, is considered to be the most excellent devotee."

ARJUNA:

"O slayer of Madhu, on account of the restlessness of the mind, I do not perceive any possibility of steady continuance in this yoga of equanimity which thou hast declared. For indeed, O Krishna, the mind is full of agitation, turbulent, strong, and obstinate. I believe the restraint of it to be as difficult as that of the wind."

KRISHNA:

"Without doubt, O thou of mighty arms, the mind is restless and hard to restrain; but it may be restrained, O son of Kunti, by practice and absence of desire. Yet in my opinion this divine discipline called yoga is very difficult for one who hath not his soul in his own control; yet it may be acquired through proper means and by one who is assiduous and controlleth his heart."

ARJUNA:

"What end, O Krishna, doth that man attain who, although having faith, hath not attained to perfection in his devotion because his unsubdued mind wandered from the discipline? Doth he, fallen from both , like a broken cloud without any support, become destroyed, O strong-armed one, being deluded in the path of the Supreme Spirit? Thou, Krishna, shouldst completely dispel this doubt for me, for there is none other to be found able to remove it."

KRISHNA:

"Such a man, O son of Pritha, doth not perish here or hereafter. For never to an evil place goeth one who doeth good. The man whose devotion has been broken off by death goeth to the regions of the righteous, where he dwells for an immensity of years and is then born again on earth in a pure and fortunate family; or even in a family of those who are spiritually illuminated. But such a rebirth into this life as this last is more difficult to obtain. Being thus born again he comes in contact with the knowledge which belonged to him in his former body, and from that time he struggles more diligently towards perfection, O son of Kuru. For even unwittingly, by reason of that past practice, he is led and works on. Even if only a mere enquirer, he reaches beyond the word of the *Vedas*. But the devotee who, striving with all his might, obtaineth perfection because of efforts continued through many births, goeth to the supreme goal. The man of meditation as thus described is superior to the man of penance and to the man of learning and also to the man of action; wherefore, O Arjuna, resolve thou to become a man of meditation. But of all devotees he is considered by me as the most devoted who, with heart fixed on me, full of faith, worships me."

CHAPTER VII

SPIRITUAL DISCERNMENT

KRISHNA:

"Hear, O son of Pritha, how with heart fixed on me, practicing meditation and taking me as thy refuge, thou shalt know me completely. I will instruct thee fully in this knowledge and in its realization, which, having learned, there remains nothing else to be known.

"Among thousands of mortals a single one perhaps strives for perfection, and among those so striving perhaps a single one knows me as I am. Earth, water, fire, air, and akasa, Manas, Buddhi, and Ahankara is the eightfold division of my nature. It is inferior; know that my superior nature is different and is the knower; by it the universe is sustained; learn that the whole of creation springs from this too as from a womb; I am the cause, I am the production and the dissolution of the whole universe. There is none superior to me, O conqueror of wealth, and all things hang on me as precious gems upon a string. I am the taste in water, O son of Kunti, the light in the sun and moon, the mystic syllable OM in all the *Vedas,* sound in space, the masculine essence in men, the sweet smell in the earth, and the brightness in the fire. In all creatures I am the life, and the power of concentration in those whose minds are on the spirit. Know me, O son of Pritha, as the eternal seed of all creatures. I am the wisdom of the wise and the strength of the strong. And I am the power of the strong who in action are free from desire and longing; in all creatures I am desire regulated by moral fitness. Know also that the dispositions arising from the three qualities, *sattva, rajas,* and *tamas,* are from me; they are in me, but I am not in them. The whole world, being deluded by these dispositions which are born of the three qualities, knoweth not me distinct from them, supreme, imperishable. For this my divine illusive power, acting through the natural qualities, is difficult to surmount, and those only can surmount it who have recourse to me alone. The wicked among men, the deluded and the low-minded, deprived of spiritual perception by this illusion, and inclining toward demoniacal dispositions, do not have recourse to me.

"Four classes of men who work righteousness worship me, O Arjuna; those who are afflicted, the searchers for truth, those who desire possessions, and the wise, O son of Bharata. Of these the best is the one possessed of spiritual knowledge, who is always devoted to me. I am extremely dear to the wise man, and he is dear unto me. Excellent indeed are all these, but the spiritually wise is verily myself, because with heart at peace he is upon the road that leadeth to the highest path, which is even myself. After many births the spiritually wise findeth me as the Vasudeva who is all this, for such an one of great soul is difficult to meet. Those who through diversity of desires are deprived of spiritual wisdom adopt particular rites subordinated to their own natures, and worship other Gods. In whatever form a devotee desires with faith to worship, it is I alone who inspire him with constancy therein, and depending on that faith he seeks the propitiation of that God, obtaining the object of his wishes as is ordained by me alone. But the reward of such short-sighted men is temporary. Those who worship the Gods go to the Gods, and those who worship me come unto me. The ignorant, being unacquainted with my supreme condition which is superior to all things and exempt from decay, believe me who am umnanifested to exist in a visible form. Enveloped by my magic illusion I am not visible to the world; therefore the world doth not recognize me the unborn and exhaustless. I know, O Arjuna, all creatures that have been, that are present, as well as all that shall hereafter be, but no one knows me. At the time of birth, O son of Bharata, all beings fall into error by reason of the delusion of the opposites which springs from liking and disliking, O harasser of thy foes. But those men of righteous lives whose sins have ceased, being free from this delusion of the 'pairs of opposites,' firmly settled in faith, worship me. They who depend on me, and labor for deliverance from birth and death know Brahman, the whole Adhyatma, and all Karma. Those who rest in me, knowing me to be the Adhibhuta, the Adhidaiva, and the Adhiyajna, know me also at the time of death."

CHAPTER VIII

OMNIPRESENT SPIRIT NAMED AS OM

ARJUNA:

"What is that Brahman, what is Adhyatma, and what, O best of men! is Karma? What also is Adhibhuta, and what Adhidaiva? Who too is Adhiyajna here, in this body, and how therein, O slayer of Madhu? Tell me also how men who are fixed in meditation are to know thee at the hour of death."

KRISHNA:

"Brahman the Supreme is the exhaustless. Adhyatma is the name of my being manifesting as the Individual Self. Karma is the emanation which causes the existence and reproduction of creatures. Adhibhuta is the Supreme Spirit dwelling in all elemental nature through the mysterious power of nature's illusion. Adhidaiva is the Purusha, the Spiritual Person, and Adhiyajna is myself in this body, O best of embodied men. Whoever at the hour of death abandoneth the body, fixed in meditation upon me, without doubt goeth to me. Whoso in consequence of constant meditation on any particular form thinketh upon it when quitting his mortal shape, even to that doth he go, O son of Kuni. Therefore at all times meditate only on me and fight. Thy mind and Buddhi being placed on me alone, thou shalt without doubt come to me. The man whose heart abides in me alone, wandering to no other object, shall also by meditation on the Supreme Spirit go to it, O son of Pritha. Whosoever shall meditate upon the All-Wise which is without beginning, the Supreme Ruler, the smallest of the small, the Supporter of all, whose form is incomprehensible, bright as the sun beyond the darkness; with mind undeviating, united to devotion, and by the power of meditation concentrated at the hour of death, with his vital powers placed between the eyebrows, attains to that Supreme Divine Spirit.

"I will now make known to thee that path which the learned in the *Vedas* call indestructible, into which enter those who are free from attachments, and is followed by those desirous of leading the life of a Brahmachari laboring for salvation. He who closeth all the doors of his senses, imprisoneth his mind in his heart, fixeth his vital powers in his head, standing firm in meditation, repeating the monosyllable OM, and thus continues when he is quitting the body, goeth to the supreme goal. He who, with heart undiverted to any other object, meditates constantly and through the whole of life on me shall surely attain to me, O son of Pritha. Those great-souled ones who have attained to supreme perfection come unto me and no more incur rebirths rapidly revolving, which are mansions of pain and sorrow.

"All worlds up to that of Brahman are subject to rebirth again and again, but they, O son of Kunti, who reach to me have no rebirth. Those who are acquainted with day and night know that the day of Brahma is a thousand revolutions of the yugas and that his night extendeth for a thousand more. At the coming on of that day all things issue forth from the unmanifested into manifestation, so on the approach of that night they merge again into the unmanifested. This collection of existing things, having thus come forth, is dissolved at the approach of the night, O son of Pritha; and now again on the coming of the day it emanates spontaneously. But there is that which upon the dissolution of all things else is not destroyed; it is indivisible, indestructible, and of another nature from the visible. That called the unmanifested and exhaustless is called the supreme goal, which having once attained they never more return -- it is my supreme abode. This Supreme, O son of Pritha, within whom all creatures are included and by whom all this is pervaded, may be attained by a devotion which is intent on him alone.

"I will now declare to thee, O best of the Bharatas, at what time yogis dying obtain freedom from or subjection to rebirth. Fire, light, day, the fortnight of the waxing moon, six months of the sun's northern course -- going then and knowing the Supreme Spirit, men go to the Supreme. But those who depart in smoke, at night, during the fortnight of the waning moon, and while the sun is in the path of his southern journey, proceed for a while to the regions of the moon and again return to mortal birth. These two, *light* and *darkness*, are the world's eternal ways; by one a man goes not to return, by the other he cometh back again upon earth. No devotee, O son of Pritha, who knoweth these two paths is ever deluded; wherefore, O Arjuna, at all times be thou fixed in devotion. The man of meditation who knoweth all this reaches beyond whatever rewards are promised in the *Vedas* or that result from sacrifices or austerities or from gifts of charity, and goeth to the supreme, the highest place."

36

CHAPTER IX

THE KINGLY KNOWLEDGE AND THE KINGLY MYSTERY

KRISHNA:

"Unto thee who findest no fault I will now make known this most mysterious knowledge, coupled with a realization of it, which having known thou shalt be delivered from evil. This is the royal knowledge, the royal mystery, the most excellent purifier, clearly comprehensible, not opposed to sacred law, easy to perform, and inexhaustible. Those who are unbelievers in this truth, O harasser of thy foes, find me not, but revolving in rebirth return to this world, the mansion of death.

"All this universe is pervaded by me in my invisible form; all things exist in me, but I do not exist in them. Nor are all things in me; behold this my divine mystery: myself causing things to exist and supporting them all but dwelling not in them. Understand that all things are in me even as the mighty air which passes everywhere is in space. O son of Kunti, at the end of a kalpa all things return unto my nature, and then again at the beginning of another kalpa I cause them to evolve again. Taking control of my own nature I emanate again and again this whole assemblage of beings, without their will, by the power of the material essence. These acts do not bind me, O conqueror of wealth, because I am as one who sitteth indifferent, uninterested in those works. By reason of my supervision nature produceth the animate and inanimate universe; it is through this cause, O son of Kunti, that the universe revolveth.

"The deluded despise me in human form, being unacquainted with my real nature as Lord of all things. They are of vain hopes, deluded in action, in reason and in knowledge, inclining to demoniac and deceitful principles. But those great of soul, partaking of the godlike nature, knowing me to be the imperishable principle of all things, worship me, diverted to nothing else. Fixed in unbroken vows they worship, everywhere proclaiming me and bowing down to me. Others with the sacrifice of knowledge in other ways worship me as indivisible, as separable, as the Spirit of the universe. I am the sacrifice and sacrificial rite; I am the libation offered to ancestors, and the spices; I am the sacred formula and the fire; I am the food and the sacrificial butter; I am the father and the mother of this universe, the grandsire and the preserver; I am the Holy One, the object of knowledge, the mystic purifying syllable OM, the *Rik*, the *Sama*, the *Yajur*, and all the *Vedas*. I am the goal, the Comforter, the Lord, the Witness, the resting-place, the asylum and the Friend; I am the origin and the dissolution, the receptacle, the storehouse, and the eternal seed. I cause light and heat and rain; I now draw in and now let forth; I am death and immortality; I am the cause unseen and the visible effect. Those enlightened in the three *Vedas*, offering sacrifices to me and obtaining sanctification from drinking the soma juice, petition me for heaven; thus they attain the region of Indra, the prince of celestial beings, and there feast upon celestial food and are gratified with heavenly enjoyments. And they, having enjoyed that spacious heaven for a period in proportion to their merits, sink back into this mortal world where they are born again as soon as their stock of merit is exhausted; thus those who long for the accomplishment of desires, following the *Vedas*, obtain a happiness which comes and goes. But for those who, thinking of me as identical with all, constantly worship me, I bear the burden of the responsibility of their happiness. And even those also who worship other gods with a firm faith in doing so, involuntarily worship me, too, O son of Kunti, albeit in ignorance. I am he who is the Lord of all sacrifices, and am also their enjoyer, but they do not understand me truly and therefore they fall from heaven. Those who devote themselves to the gods go to the gods; the worshipers of the pitris go to the pitris; those who worship the evil spirits go to them, and my worshipers come to me. I accept and enjoy the offerings of the humble soul who in his worship with a pure heart offereth a leaf, a flower, or fruit, or water unto me. Whatever thou doest, O son of Kunti, whatever thou eatest, whatever thou sacrificest, whatever thou givest, whatever mortification thou performest, commit each unto me. Thus thou shalt be delivered from the good and evil experiences which are the bonds of action; and thy heart being joined to renunciation and to the practice of action, thou shalt come to me. I am the same to all creatures; I know not hatred nor favor; but those who serve me with love dwell in me and I in them. Even if the man of most evil ways worship me with exclusive devotion, he is to be considered as righteous, for he hath judged aright. Such a man soon becometh of a righteous soul and obtaineth perpetual happiness. I swear, O son of Kunti, that he who worships me never perisheth. Those even who may be of the womb of sin, women, vaisyas, and sudras, shall tread the highest path if they take sanctuary with me. How much more, then, holy brahmans and devotees of kingly race! Having obtained this finite, joyless world, worship me. Serve me, fix heart and mind on me, be my servant, my adorer, prostrate thyself before me, and thus, united unto me, at rest, thou shalt go unto me."

CHAPTER X

THE UNIVERSAL DIVINE PERFECTIONS

KRISHNA:

"Hear again, O thou of mighty arms, my supreme words, which unto thee who art well pleased I will declare because I am anxious for thy welfare.

"Neither the assemblage of the Gods nor the Adept Kings know my origin, because I am the origin of all the Gods and of the Adepts. Whosoever knoweth me to be the mighty Ruler of the universe and without birth or beginning, he among men, undeluded, shall be liberated from all his sins. Subtle perception, spiritual knowledge, right judgment, patience, truth, self-mastery; pleasure and pain, prosperity and adversity; birth and death, danger and security, fear and equanimity, satisfaction, restraint of body and mind, alms-giving, inoffensiveness, zeal and glory and ignominy, all these the various dispositions of creatures come from me. So in former days the seven great Sages and the four Manus who are of my nature were born of my mind, and from them sprang this world. He who knoweth perfectly this permanence and mystic faculty of mine becometh without doubt possessed of unshaken faith. I am the origin of all; all things proceed from me; believing me to be thus, the wise gifted with spiritual wisdom worship me; their very hearts and minds are in me; enlightening one another and constantly speaking of me, they are full of enjoyment and satisfaction. To them thus always devoted to me, who worship me with love, I give that mental devotion by which they come to me. For them do I out of my compassion, standing within their hearts, destroy the darkness which springs from ignorance by the brilliant lamp of spiritual discernment."

ARJUNA:

"Thou art Parabrahman! the supreme abode, the great Purification; thou art the Eternal Presence, the Divine Being, before all other Gods, holy, primeval, all-pervading, without beginning! Thus thou art declared by all the Sages -- by Narada, Asita, Devala, Vyasa, and thou thyself now dost say the same. I firmly believe all that thou, O Kesava, sayest unto me; for neither Gods nor demons comprehend thy manifestations. Thou alone knowest thyself by thy Self, Supreme Spirit, Creator and Master of all that lives, God of Gods, and Lord of all the universe! Thou alone canst fully declare thy divine powers by which thou hast pervaded and continuest to pervade these worlds. How shall 1, constantly thinking of thee, be able to know thee, O mysterious Lord? In what particular forms shall I meditate on thee? O Janardana -- besought by mortals -- tell me therefore in full thine own powers and forms of manifestation, for I am never sated of drinking of the life-giving water of thy words."

KRISHNA:

"O best of Kurus, blessings be upon thee. I will make thee acquainted with the chief of my divine manifestations, for the extent of my nature is infinite.

"I am the Ego which is seated in the hearts of all beings; I am the beginning, the middle, and the end of all existing things. Among Adityas I am Vishnu, and among luminous bodies I am the sun. I am Marichi among the Maruts , and among heavenly mansions I am the moon. Among the *Vedas* I am the *Samaveda* ,and Indra among the Gods; among the senses and organs I am the Manas , and of creatures the existence. I am Sankara among the Rudras; and Vittesa, the lord of wealth among the Yakshas and Rakshasas. I am Pavaka among the Vasus, and Meru among high-aspiring mountains. And know, O son of Pritha, that I am Brihaspati, the chief of teachers; among leaders of celestial armies Skanda, and of floods I am the ocean. I am Bhrigu among the Adept Kings; of words I am the monosyllable OM; of forms of worship, the silent repetition of sacred texts, and of immovable things I am the Himalaya. Of all the trees of the forest I am Asvattha the Pippala tree; and of the celestial Sages, Narada; among Gandharvas I am Chitraratha, and of perfect saints, Kapila. Know that among horses I am Uchchaisrava, who arose with the Amrita out of the ocean; among elephants, Airavata, and among men their sovereigns. Of weapons I am the thunderbolt; among cows, Kamadhuk, the cow of plenty; of procreators, the God of love, and of serpents, Vasuki, their chief. I am Ananta among the Nagas, Varuna among things of the waters; among the ancestors, Aryarman, and of all who judge I am Yama. Among the Daityas I am Prahlada, and among computations I am Time itself; the lion among beasts, and Garuda among the feathered tribe. Among purifiers I am Pavana, the air; Rama among those who carry arms, Makara among the fishes, and the Ganges among rivers. Among that which is evolved, O Arjuna, I am the beginning, the middle, and the end; of all sciences I am the knowledge of the Adhyatma , and of uttered sounds the human speech. Among letters I am the vowel A, and of all compound words I am the Dvandva ; I am endless time itself, and the Preserver whose face is turned on all sides. I am all-grasping death, and the birth of those who are to be; among feminine things I am fame, fortune, speech, memory, intelligence, patience, and forgiveness. Among the hymns of the *Samaveda* I am *Brihat-Saman,* and the Gayatri among metres; among months I am the month Margasirsha, and of seasons spring called Kusumakara, the time of flowers. Of those things which deceive I am the dice, and splendor itself among splendid things. I am victory, I am perseverance, and the goodness of the good. Of the race of Vrishni I am Vasudeva; of the Pandava I am Arjuna the conqueror of wealth; of perfect saints I am Vyasa, and of prophet-seers I am the bard Usana. Among rulers I am the rod of punishment, among those desiring conquest I am policy; and among the wise of secret knowledge I am their silence. I am, O Arjuna, the seed of all existing things, and there is not anything, whether animate or inanimate which is without me. My divine manifestations, O harasser of thy foes, are without end, the many which I have mentioned are by way of example. Whatever creature is permanent, of good fortune or mighty, also know it to be sprung from a portion of my energy. But what, O Arjuna, hast thou to do with so much knowledge as this? I established this whole universe with a single portion of myself, and remain separate."

CHAPTER XI

THE VISION OF THE DIVINE FORM AS INCLUDING ALL FORMS

ARJUNA:

"My delusion has been dispersed by the words which thou for my soul's peace hast spoken concerning the mystery of the Adhyatma -- the spirit. For I have heard at full length from thee, O thou whose eyes are like lotus leaves, the origin and dissolution of existing things, and also thy inexhaustible majesty. It is even as thou hast described thyself, O mighty Lord; I now desire to see thy divine form, O sovereign Lord. Wherefore, O Lord, if thou thinkest it may be beheld by me, show me, O Master of devotion, thine inexhaustible Self."

KRISHNA:

"Behold, O son of Pritha, my forms by hundreds and by thousands, of diverse kinds divine, of many shapes and fashions. Behold the Adityas, Vasus, Rudras, Asvins, and the Maruts, see things wonderful never seen before, O son of Bharata. Here in my body now behold, O Gudakesa, the whole universe animate and inanimate gathered here in one, and all things else thou hast a wish to see. But as with thy natural eyes thou are not able to see me, I will give thee the divine eye. Behold my sovereign power and might!"

SANJAYA:

O king, having thus spoken, Hari, the mighty Lord of mysterious power, showed to the son of Pritha his supreme form; with many mouths and eyes and many wonderful appearances, with many divine ornaments, many celestial weapons upraised; adorned with celestial garlands and robes, anointed with celestial ointments and perfumes, full of every marvelous thing, the eternal God whose face is turned in all directions. The glory and amazing splendor of this mighty Being may be likened to the radiance shed by a thousand suns rising together into the heavens. The son of Pandu then beheld within the body of the God of gods the whole universe in all its vast variety. Overwhelmed with wonder, Dhananjaya, the possessor of wealth, with hair standing on end, bowed down his head before the Deity, and thus with joined palms addressed him:

ARJUNA:

"I behold, O God of gods, within thy frame all beings and things of every kind; the Lord Brahma on his lotus throne, all the Rishis and the heavenly Serpents. I see thee on all sides, of infinite forms, having many arms, stomachs, mouths, and eyes. But I can discover neither thy beginning, thy middle, nor thy end, O universal Lord, form of the universe. I see thee crowned with a diadem and armed with mace and chakra, a mass of splendor, darting light on all sides; difficult to behold, shining in every direction with light immeasurable, like the burning fire or glowing sun. Thou art the supreme inexhaustible Being, the end of effort, changeless, the Supreme Spirit of this universe, the never-failing guardian of eternal law: I esteem thee Purusha, I see thee without beginning middle, or end, of infinite power with arms innumerable, the sun and moon thy eyes, thy mouth a flaming fire, overmastering the whole universe with thy majesty. Space and heaven, and earth and every point around the three regions of the universe are filled with thee alone. The triple world is full of fear, O thou mighty Spirit, seeing this thy marvelous form of terror. Of the assemblage of the gods some I see fly to thee for refuge, while some in fear with joined hands sing forth thy praise; the hosts of the Maharshis and Siddhas, great sages and saints, hail thee, saying "svasti," and glorify thee with most excellent hymns. The Rudras, Adityas, the Vasus, and all those beings -- the Sadhyas, Visvas, the Asvins, Maruts, and Ushmapas, the hosts of Gandharvas, Yakshas, and Siddhas -- all stand gazing on thee and are amazed. All the worlds alike with me are terrified to behold thy wondrous form gigantic, O thou of mighty arms, with many mouths and eyes, with many arms, thighs and feet, with many stomachs and projecting tusks. For seeing thee thus touching the heavens, shining with such glory, with widely-opened mouths and bright expanded eyes, my inmost soul is troubled and I lose both firmness and tranquillity, O Vishnu. Beholding thy dreadful teeth and thy face like the burning of death, I can see neither heaven nor earth; I find no peace; have mercy, O Lord of gods, thou Spirit of the universe! The sons of Dhritarashtra with all these rulers of men, Bhishma, Drona and also Kama and our principal warriors, seem to be impetuously precipitating themselves into thy mouths terrible with tusks; some are seen caught between thy teeth, their heads ground down. As the rapid streams of full-flowing rivers roll on to meet the ocean, even so these heroes of the human race rush into thy flaming mouths. As troops of insects carried away by strong impulse find death in the fire, even so do these beings with swelling force pour into thy mouths for their own destruction. Thou involvest and swallowest all these creatures from every side, licking them in thy flaming lips; filling the universe with thy splendor, thy sharp beams burn, O Vishnu. Reverence be unto thee, O best of Gods! Be favorable! I seek to know thee, the Primeval One, for I know not thy work."

KRISHNA:

"I am Time matured, come hither for the destruction of these creatures; except thyself, not one of all these warriors here drawn up in serried ranks shall live. Wherefore, arise! seize fame! Defeat the foe and enjoy the fullgrown kingdom! They have been already slain by me; be thou only the immediate agent, O thou both-armed one. Be not disturbed. Slay Drona, Bhishma, Jayadratha, Karna, and all the other heroes of the war who are really slain by me. Fight, thou wilt conquer all thine enemies."

SANJAYA:

When he of the resplendent diadem heard these words from the mouth of Kesava , he saluted Krishna with joined palms and trembling with fear, addressed him in broken accents, and bowed down terrified before him.

ARJUNA:

"The universe, O Hrishikesa, is justly delighted with thy glory and is filled with zeal for thy service; the evil spirits are affrighted and flee on all sides, while all the hosts of saints bow down in adoration before thee. And wherefore should they not adore thee, O mighty Being, thou who art greater than Brahma, who art the first Maker? O eternal God of gods! O habitation of the universe! Thou art the one indivisible Being, and Non-Being, that which is supreme. Thou art the first of Gods, the most ancient Spirit; thou art the final supreme receptacle of this universe; thou art the Knower and that which is to be known, and the supreme mansion; and by thee, O thou of infinite form, is this universe caused to emanate. Thou art Vayu, God of wind, Agni, God of fire, Yama, God of death, Varuna, God of waters; thou art the moon; Prajapati, the progenitor and grandfather, art thou. Hail! hail to thee! Hail to thee a thousand times repeated! Again and again hail to thee! Hail to thee! Hail to thee from before! Hail to thee from behind! Hail to thee on all sides, O thou All! Infinite is thy power and might; thou includest all things, therefore thou art all things!

"Having been ignorant of thy majesty, I took thee for a friend, and have called thee 'O Krishna, O son of Yadu, O friend,' and blinded by my affection and presumption, I have at times treated thee without respect in sport, in recreation, in repose, in thy chair, and at thy meals, in private and in public; all this I beseech thee, O inconceivable Being, to forgive.

"Thou art the father of all things animate and inanimate; thou art to be honored as above the guru himself, and worthy to be adored; there is none equal to thee, and how in the triple worlds could there be thy superior, O thou of unrivaled power? Therefore I bow down and with my body prostrate, I implore thee, O Lord, for mercy. Forgive, O Lord, as the friend forgives the friend, as the father pardons his son, as the lover the beloved. I am well pleased with having beheld what was never before seen, and yet my heart is overwhelmed with awe; have mercy then, O God; show me that other form, O thou who art the dwelling-place of the universe; I desire to see thee as before with thy diadem on thy head, thy hands armed with mace and chakra; assume again, O thou of a thousand arms and universal form, thy four-armed shape!"

KRISHNA:

"Out of kindness to thee, O Arjuna, by my divine power I have shown thee my supreme form, the universe, resplendent, infinite, primeval, and which has never been beheld by any other than thee. Neither by studying the *Vedas,* nor by alms-giving, nor by sacrificial rites, nor by deeds, nor by the severest mortification of the flesh can I be seen in this form by any other than thee, O best of Kurus. Having beheld my form thus awful, be not disturbed nor let thy faculties be confounded, but with fears allayed and happiness of heart look upon this other form of mine again."

SANJAYA:

Vasudeva having so spoken reassumed his natural form; and thus in milder shape the Great One presently assuaged the fears of the terrified Arjuna.

ARJUNA:

"Now that I see again thy placid human shape, O Janadana, who art prayed to by mortals, my mind is no more disturbed and I am self-possessed."

KRISHNA:

"Thou hast seen this form of mine which is difficult to be perceived and which even the gods arc always anxious to behold. But I am not to be seen, even as I have shown myself to thee, by study of the *Vedas,* nor by mortifications, nor alms-giving, nor sacrifices. I am to be approached and seen and known in truth by means of that devotion which has me alone as the object. He whose actions are for me alone, who esteemeth me the supreme goal, who is my servant only, without attachment to the results of action and free from enmity towards any creature, cometh to me, O son of Pandu."

CHAPTER XII

DEVOTION BY MEANS OF FAITH

ARJUNA:

"Among those of thy devotees who always thus worship thee, which take the better way, those who worship the indivisible and unmanifested, or those who serve thee as thou now art?"

KRISHNA:

"Those who worship me with constant zeal, with the highest faith and minds placed on me, are held in high esteem by me. But those who, with minds equal toward everything, with senses and organs restrained, and rejoicing in the good of all creatures, meditate on the inexhaustible, immovable, highest, incorruptible, difficult to contemplate, invisible, omnipresent, unthinkable, the witness, undemonstrable, shall also come unto me. For those whose hearts are fixed on the unmanifested the labor is greater because the path which is not manifest is with difficulty attained by corporeal beings. But for those who worship me, renouncing in me all their actions, regarding me as the supreme goal and meditating on me alone, if their thoughts are turned to me, O son of Pritha, I presently become the savior from this ocean of incarnations and death. Place, then, thy heart on me, penetrate me with thy understanding, and thou shalt without doubt hereafter dwell in me. But if thou shouldst be unable at once steadfastly to fix thy heart and mind on me, strive then, O Dhananjaya, to find me by constant practice in devotion. If after constant practice, thou art still unable, follow me by actions performed for me; for by doing works for me thou shalt attain perfection. But if thou art unequal even to this, then, being self-restrained, place all thy works, failures and successes alike, on me, abandoning in me the fruit of every action. For knowledge is better than constant practice, meditation is superior to knowledge, renunciation of the fruit of action to meditation; final emancipation immediately results from such renunciation.

"My devotee who is free from enmity, well-disposed towards all creatures, merciful, wholly exempt from pride and selfishness, the same in pain and pleasure, patient of wrongs, contented, constantly devout, self-governed, firm in resolves, and whose mind and heart are fixed on me alone, is dear unto me. He also is my beloved of whom mankind is not afraid and who has no fear of man; who is free from joy, from despondency and the dread of harm. My devotee who is unexpecting, pure, just, impartial, devoid of fear, and who hath forsaken interest in the results of action, is dear unto me. He also is worthy of my love who neither rejoiceth nor findeth fault, who neither lamenteth nor coveteth, and being my servant hath forsaken interest in both good and evil results. He also is my beloved servant who is equal-minded to friend or foe, the same in honor and dishonor, in cold and heat, in pain and pleasure, and is unsolicitous about the event of things; to whom praise and blame are as one; who is of little speech, content with whatever cometh to pass, who hath no fixed habitation, and whose heart, full of devotion, is firmly fixed. But those who seek this sacred ambrosia -- the religion of immortality -- even as I have explained it, full of faith, intent on me above all others, and united to devotion, are my most beloved."

CHAPTER XIII

THE DISCRIMINATION OF THE KSHETRA FROM KSHETRAJNA

KRISHNA:

"This perishable body, O son of Kunti, is known as Kshetra; those who are acquainted with the true nature of things call the soul who knows it, the Kshetrajna. Know also that I am the Knower in every mortal body, O son of Bharata; that knowledge which through the soul is a realization of both the known and the knower is alone esteemed by me as wisdom. What the Kshetra or body is, what it resembleth, what it produceth, and what is its origin, and also who he is who, dwelling within, knoweth it, as well as what is his power, learn all in brief from me. It has been manifoldly sung by the Rishis with discrimination and with arguments in the various Vedic hymns which treat of Brahman.

"This body, then, is made up of the great elements, Ahankara -- egotism, Buddhi -- intellect or judgment, the unmanifest, invisible spirit; the ten centers of action, the mind, and the five objects of sense; desire, aversion, pleasure and pain, persistency of life, and firmness, the power of cohesion. Thus I have made known unto thee what the Kshetra or body is with its component parts.

"True wisdom of a spiritual kind is freedom from self-esteem, hypocrisy, and injury to others; it is patience, sincerity, respect for spiritual instructors, purity, firmness, self-restraint, dispassion for objects of sense, freedom from pride, and a meditation upon birth, death, decay, sickness, and error; it is an exemption from self-identifying attachment for children, wife, and household, and a constant unwavering steadiness of heart upon the arrival of every event whether favorable or unfavorable; it is a never-ceasing love for me alone, the self being effaced, and worship paid in a solitary spot, and a want of pleasure in congregations of men; it is a resolute continuance in the study of Adhyatma, the Superior spirit, and a meditation upon the end

51

of the acquirement of a knowledge of truth; -- this is called wisdom or spiritual knowledge; its opposite is ignorance.

"I will now tell thee what is the object of wisdom, from knowing which a man enjoys immortality; it is that which has no beginning, even the supreme Brahman, and of which it cannot be said that it is either Being or Non-Being. It has hands and feet in all directions; eyes, heads, mouths, and ears in every direction; it is immanent in the world, possessing the vast whole. Itself without organs, it is reflected by all the senses and faculties; unattached, yet supporting all; without qualities, yet the witness of them all. It is within and without all creatures animate and inanimate; it is inconceivable because of its subtlety, and although near it is afar off. Although undivided it appeareth as divided among creatures, and while it sustains existing things, it is also to be known as their destroyer and creator. It is the light of all lights, and is declared to be beyond all darkness; and it is wisdom itself, the object of wisdom, and that which is to be obtained by wisdom; in the hearts of all it ever presideth. Thus hath been briefly declared what is the perishable body, and wisdom itself, together with the object of wisdom; he, my devotee, who thus in truth conceiveth me, obtaineth my state.

"Know that *prakriti* or nature, and *purusha* the spirit, are without beginning. And know that the passions and the three qualities are sprung from nature. Nature or *prakriti* is said to be that which operates in producing cause and effect in actions; individual spirit or *purusha* is said to be the cause of experiencing pain and pleasure. For spirit when invested with matter or *prakriti* experienceth the qualities which proceed from *prakriti*; its connection with these qualities is the cause of its rebirth in good and evil wombs. The spirit in the body is called *Mahesvara,* the Great Lord, the spectator, the admonisher, the sustainer, the enjoyer, and also the *Paramatma*, the highest soul. He who thus knoweth the spirit and nature, together with the qualities, whatever mode of life he may lead, is not born again on this earth.

"Some men by meditation, using contemplation upon the Self, behold the spirit within, others attain to that end by philosophical study with its realization, and others by means of the religion of works. Others, again, who are not acquainted with it in this manner, but have heard it from others, cleave unto and respect it; and even these, if assiduous only upon tradition and attentive to hearing the scriptures, pass beyond the gulf of death.

"Know, O chief of the Bharatas, that whenever anything, whether animate or inanimate, is produced, it is due to the union of the Kshetra and Kshetrajna -- body and the soul. He who seeth the Supreme Being existing alike imperishable in all perishable things, sees indeed. Perceiving the same Lord present in everything and everywhere, he does not by the lower self destroy his own soul, but goeth to the supreme end. He who seeth that all his actions are performed by nature only, and that the self within is not the actor, sees indeed. And when he realizes perfectly that all things whatsoever in nature are comprehended in the ONE, he attains to the Supreme Spirit. This Supreme Spirit, O son of Kunti, even when it is in the body, neither acteth nor is it affected by action, because, being without beginning and devoid of attributes, it is changeless. As the all-moving Akasa by reason of its subtlety passeth everywhere unaffected, so the Spirit, though present in every kind of body, is not attached to action nor affected. As a single sun illuminateth the whole world, even so doth the One Spirit illumine every body, O son of Bharata. Those who with the eye of wisdom thus perceive what is the difference between the body and Spirit and the destruction of the illusion of objects, go to the Supreme."

CHAPTER XIV

SEPARATION FROM THE THREE QUALITIES

KRISHNA:

"I will explain further the sublime spiritual knowledge superior to all others, by knowing which all the sages have attained to supreme perfection on the dissolution of this body. They take sanctuary in this wisdom, and having attained to my state they are not born again even at the new evolution, nor are they disturbed at the time of general destruction.

"The great Brahman is my womb in which I place the seed; from that, O son of Bharata, is the production of all existing things. This great Brahman is the womb for all those various forms which are produced from any womb, and I am the Father who provideth the seed. The three great qualities called *sattva, rajas*, and *tamas* -- light, or truth, passion or desire, and indifference or darkness -- are born from nature, and bind the imperishable soul to the body, O thou of mighty arms. Of these the *sattva* quality by reason of its lucidity and peacefulness entwineth the soul to rebirth through attachment to knowledge and that which is pleasant. Know that *rajas* is of the nature of desire, producing thirst and propensity; it, O son of Kunti, imprisoneth the Ego through the consequences produced from action. The quality of *tamas,* the offspring of the indifference in nature, is the deluder of all creatures, O son of Bharata; it imprisoneth the Ego in a body through heedless folly, sleep, and idleness. The *sattva* quality attaches the soul through happiness and pleasure, the *rajas* through action, and *tamas* quality surrounding the power of judgment with indifference attaches the soul through heedlessness.

"When, O son of Bharata, the qualities of *tamas* and *rajas* are overcome, then that of *sattva* prevaileth;*tamas* is chiefly acting when *sattva* and *rajas* are hidden; and when the *sattva* and *tamas* diminish, then *rajas* prevaileth. When wisdom, the bright light, shall become

55

evident at every gate of the body, then one may know that the *sattva* quality is prevalent within. The love of gain, activity in action, and the initiating of works, restlessness and inordinate desire are produced when the quality of *rajas* is prevalent, whilst the tokens of the predominance of the *tamas* quality are absence of illumination, the presence of idleness, heedlessness, and delusion, O son of Kunti.

"If the body is dissolved when the *sattva* quality prevails, the self within proceeds to the spotless spheres of those who are acquainted with the highest place. When the body is dissolved while the quality of *rajas* is predominant, the soul is born again in a body attached to action; and so also of one who dies while *tamas* quality is prevalent, the soul is born again in the wombs of those who are deluded.

"The fruit of righteous acts is called pure and holy, appertaining to *sattva*; from *rajas* is gathered fruit in pain, and the *tamas* produceth only senselessness, ignorance, and indifference. From *sattva* wisdom is produced, from *rajas* desire, from *tamas* ignorance, delusion and folly. Those in whom the *sattva* quality is established mount on high, those who are full of *rajas* remain in the middle sphere, the world of men, while those who are overborne by the gloomy quality, *tamas*, sink below. But when the wise man perceiveth that the only agents of action are these qualities, and comprehends that which is superior to the qualities, he attains to my state. And when the embodied self surpasseth these three qualities of goodness, action, and indifference -- which are coexistent with the body -- it is released from rebirth and death, old age and pain, and drinketh of the water of immortality."

ARJUNA:

"What are the characteristic marks by which the man may be known, O Master, who hath surpassed the three qualities? What is his course of life, and what are the means by which he overcometh the qualities?"

KRISHNA:

"He, O son of Pandu, who doth not hate these qualities -- illumination, action, and delusion -- when they appear, nor longeth for them when they disappear; who, like one who is of no party, sitteth as one unconcerned about the three qualities and undisturbed by them, who being persuaded that the qualities exist, is moved not by them; who is of equal mind in pain and pleasure, self-centered, to whom a lump of earth, a stone, or gold are as one; who is of equal mind with those who love or dislike, constant, the same whether blamed or praised; equally minded in honor and disgrace, and the same toward friendly or unfriendly side, engaging only in necessary actions, such an one hath surmounted the qualities. And he, my servant, who worships me with exclusive devotion, having completely overcome the qualities, is fitted to

56

be absorbed in Brahman the Supreme. I am the embodiment of the Supreme Ruler, and of the incorruptible, of the unmodifying, and of the eternal law, and of endless bliss."

CHAPTER XV

KNOWLEDGE OF THE SUPREME SPIRIT

KRISHNA:

"Men say that the *Asvattha*, the eternal sacred tree, grows with its roots above and its branches below, and the leaves of which are the *Vedas*; he who knows this knows the *Vedas*. Its branches growing out of the three qualities with the objects of sense as the lesser shoots, spread forth, some above and some below; and those roots which ramify below in the regions of mankind are the connecting bonds of action. Its form is not thus understood by men; it has no beginning, nor can its present constitution be understood, nor has it any end. When one hath hewn down with the strong axe of dispassion this *Asvattha* tree with its deeply-imbedded roots, then that place is to be sought after from which those who there take refuge never more return to rebirth, for it is the Primeval Spirit from which floweth the never-ending stream of conditioned existence. Those who are free from pride of self and whose discrimination is perfected, who have prevailed over the fault of attachment to action, who are constantly employed in devotion to meditation upon the Supreme Spirit, who have renounced desire and are free from the influence of the opposites known as pleasure and pain, are undeluded, and proceed to that place which endureth forever. Neither the sun nor the moon nor the fire enlighteneth that place; from it there is no return; it is my supreme abode.

"It is even a portion of myself which, having assumed life in this world of conditioned existence, draweth together the five senses and the mind in order that it may obtain a body and may leave it again. And those are carried by the Sovereign Lord to and from whatever body he enters or quits, even as the breeze bears the fragrance from the flower. Presiding over the eye, the ear, the touch, the taste, and the power of smelling, and also over the mind, he experienceth the objects of sense. The deluded do not see the spirit when it quitteth or remains in the body, nor when, moved by the qualities, it has experience in the world. But

59

those who have the eye of wisdom perceive it, and devotees who industriously strive to do so see it dwelling in their own hearts; whilst those who have not overcome themselves, who are devoid of discrimination, see it not even though they strive thereafter. Know that the brilliance of the sun which illuminateth the whole world, and the light which is in the moon and in the fire, are the splendor of myself. I enter the earth supporting all living things by my power, and I am that property of sap which is taste, nourishing all the herbs and plants of the field. Becoming the internal fire of the living, I associate with the upward and downward breathing, and cause the four kinds of food to digest. I am in the hearts of all men, and from me come memory, knowledge, and also the loss of both. I am to be known by all the *Vedas*; I am he who is the author of the *Vedanta,* and I alone am the interpreter of the *Vedas*.

"There are two kinds of beings in the world, the one divisible, the other indivisible; the divisible is all things and the creatures, the indivisible is called Kutastha, or he who standeth on high unaffected. But there is another spirit designated as the Supreme Spirit -- Paramatma -- which permeates and sustains the three worlds. As I am above the divisible and also superior to the indivisible, therefore both in the world and in the *Vedas* am I known as the Supreme Spirit. He who being not deluded knoweth me thus as the Supreme Spirit, knoweth all things and worships me under every form and condition.

"Thus, O sinless one, have I declared unto thee this most sacred science; he who understandeth it, O son of Bharata, will be a wise man and the performer of all that is to be done."

CHAPTER XVI

DISCRIMINATING BETWEEN GODLIKE AND
DEMONIACAL NATURES

KRISHNA:

"Fearlessness, sincerity, assiduity in devotion, generosity, self-restraint, piety, and alms-giving, study, mortification, and rectitude; harmlessness, veracity, and freedom from anger, resignation, equanimity, and not speaking of the faults of others, universal compassion, modesty, and mildness; patience, power, fortitude, and purity, discretion, dignity, unrevengefulness, and freedom from conceit -- these are the marks of him whose virtues are of a godlike character, O son of Bharata. Those, O son of Pritha, who are born with demoniacal dispositions are marked by hypocrisy, pride, anger, presumption, harshness of speech, and ignorance. The destiny of those whose attributes are godlike is final liberation, while that of demoniacal dispositions, born to the Asuras' lot, is continued bondage to mortal birth; grieve not, O son of Pandu, for thou art born with the divine destiny. There are two kinds of natures in beings in this world, that which is godlike, and the other which is demoniacal; the godlike hath been fully declared, hear now from me, O son of Pritha, what the demoniacal is.

"Those who are born with the demoniacal disposition -- of the nature of the Asuras -- know not the nature of action nor of cessation from action, they know not purity nor right behavior, they possess no truthfulness. They deny that the universe has any truth in it, saying it is not governed by law, declaring that it hath no Spirit; they say creatures are produced alone through the union of the sexes, and that all is for enjoyment only. Maintaining this view, their souls being ruined, their minds contracted, with natures perverted, enemies of the world, they are born to destroy. They indulge insatiable desires, are full of hypocrisy, fast-fixed in false beliefs through their delusions. They indulge in unlimited reflections which end only in annihilation, convinced until death that the enjoyment of the objects of their desires is the supreme good. Fast-bound by the hundred cords of desire, prone to lust and anger, they seek by injustice and the accumulation of wealth for the gratification of their own lusts and appetites. 'This today hath been acquired by me, and that object of my heart I shall obtain; this wealth I have, and that also shall be mine. This foe have I already slain, and others will I forthwith vanquish; I am the lord, I am powerful, and I am happy. I am rich and with precedence among men; where is there another like unto me? I shall make sacrifices, give alms, and enjoy.' In this manner do those speak who are deluded. Confounded by all manner of desires, entangled in the net of delusion, firmly attached to the gratification of their desires, they descend into hell. Esteeming themselves very highly, self-willed, full of pride and ever in pursuit of riches, they perform worship with hypocrisy and not even according to ritual, but only for outward show. Indulging in pride, selfishness, ostentation, power, lust, and anger, they detest me who am in their bodies and in the bodies of others. Wherefore I continually hurl these cruel haters, the lowest of men, into wombs of an infernal nature in this world of rebirth. And they being doomed to those infernal wombs, more and more deluded in each succeeding rebirth, never come to me, O son of Kunti, but go at length to the lowest region.

"The gates of hell are three -- desire, anger, covetousness, which destroy the soul; wherefore one should abandon them. Being free from these three gates of hell, O son of Kunti, a man worketh for the salvation of his soul, and thus proceeds to the highest path. He who abandoneth the ordinances of the Scriptures to follow the dictates of his own desires, attaineth neither perfection nor happiness nor the highest path. Therefore, in deciding what is fit and what unfit to be done, thou shouldst perform actions on earth with a knowledge of what is declared in Holy Writ."

CHAPTER XVII

THE THREE KINDS OF FAITH

ARJUNA:

"What is the state of those men who, while they neglect the precepts of the Scriptures, yet worship in faith, O Krishna? Is it of the *sattva,* the *rajas,* or the *tamas* quality?"

KRISHNA:

"The faith of mortals is of three kinds, and is born from their own disposition; it is of the quality of truth -- *sattva,* action -- *rajas,* and indifference -- *tamas;* hear now what those are.

"The faith of each one, O son of Bharata, proceeds from the *sattva* quality; the embodied soul being gifted with faith, each man is of the same nature as that ideal on which his faith is fixed. Those who are of the disposition which ariseth from the prevalence of the *sattva* or good quality worship the gods; those of the quality of *rajas* worship the celestial powers, the Yakshas and Rakshasas; other men in whom the dark quality of indifference or *tamas* predominates worship elemental powers and the ghosts of dead men. Those who practice severe self-mortification not enjoined in the Scriptures are full of hypocrisy and pride, longing for what is past and desiring more to come. They, full of delusion, torture the powers and faculties which are in the body, and me also, who am in the recesses of the innermost heart; know that they are of an infernal tendency.

"Know that food which is pleasant to each one, as also sacrifices, mortification, and alms-giving, are of three kinds; hear what their divisions are. The food which increases the length of days, vigor and strength, which keeps one free from sickness, of tranquil mind, and contented, and which is savory, nourishing, of permanent benefit and congenial to the body, is that which is attractive to those in whom the

63

sattva quality prevaileth. The food which is liked by those of the *rajas* quality is over bitter, too acid, excessively salt, hot, pungent, dry and burning, and causeth unpleasantness, pain, and disease. Whatever food is such as was dressed the day before, that is tasteless or rotting, that is impure, is that which is preferred by those in whom predominates the quality of *tamas* or indifference.

"The sacrifice or worship which is directed by Scripture and is performed by those who expect no reward but who are convinced that it is necessary to be done, is of the quality of light, of goodness, of *sattva.* But know that that worship or sacrifice which is performed with a view to its results, and also for an ostentation of piety, belongs to passion, the quality of *rajas*, O best of the Bharatas. But that which is not according to the precepts of Holy Writ, without distribution of bread, without sacred hymns, without gifts to brahmans at the conclusion, and without faith, is of the quality of *tamas.*

"Honoring the gods, the brahmans, the teachers, and the wise, purity, rectitude, chastity, and harmlessness are called mortification of the body. Gentle speech which causes no anxiety, which is truthful and friendly, and diligence in the reading of the Scriptures, are said to be austerities of speech. Serenity of mind, mildness of temper, silence, self-restraint, absolute straightforwardness of conduct, are called mortification of the mind. This threefold mortification or austerity practiced with supreme faith and by those who long not for a reward is of the *sattva* quality.

"But that austerity which is practiced with hypocrisy, for the sake of obtaining respect for oneself or for fame or favor, and which is uncertain and belonging wholly to this world, is of the quality of *rajas.* Those austerities which are practiced merely by wounding oneself or from a false judgment or for the hurting of another are of the quality of *tamas.* Those gifts which are bestowed at the proper time to the proper person, and by men who are not desirous of a return, are of the *sattva* quality, good and of the nature of truth. But that gift which is given with the expectation of a return from the beneficiary or with a view to spiritual benefit flowing therefrom or with reluctance, is of the *rajas* quality, bad and partaketh of untruth. Gifts given out of place and season and to unworthy persons, without proper attention and scornfully, are of the *tamas* quality, wholly bad and of the nature of darkness.

"OM TAT SAT: these are said to be the threefold designation of the Supreme Being. By these in the beginning were sanctified the knowers of Brahman, the *Vedas,* and sacrifices. Therefore the sacrifices, the giving of alms, and the practicing of austerities are always, among those who expound Holy Writ, preceded by the word OM. Among those who long for immortality and who do not consider the reward for their actions, the word TAT precedes their rites of sacrifice, their austerities, and giving of alms. The word SAT is used for qualities that are true and holy, and likewise is applied to laudable actions, O son of Pritha. The state of mental sacrifice when actions are at rest is also called SAT. Whatever is done without faith, whether it be sacrifice, alms-giving, or austerities, is called ASAT, that which is devoid of truth and goodness, O son of Pritha, and is not of any benefit either in this life or after death."

CHAPTER XVIII

RENUNCIATION AND FINAL LIBERATION

ARJUNA:

"I wish to learn, O great-armed one, the nature of abstaining from action and of the giving up of the results of action, and also the difference between these two, O slayer of Kesin."

KRISHNA:

"The bards conceive that the forsaking of actions which have a desired object is renunciation or Sannyasa, the wise call the disregard of the fruit of every action true disinterestedness in action. By some wise men it is said, 'Every action is as much to be avoided as a crime,' while by others it is declared, 'Deeds of sacrifice, of mortification, and of charity should not be forsaken.' Among these divided opinions hear my certain decision, O best of the Bharatas, upon this matter of disinterested forsaking, which is declared to be of three kinds, O chief of men. Deeds of sacrifice, of mortification, and of charity are not to be abandoned, for they are proper to be performed, and are the purifiers of the wise. But even those works are to be performed after having renounced all selfish interest in them and in their fruits; this, O son of Pritha, is my ultimate and supreme decision. The abstention from works which are necessary and obligatory is improper; the not doing of such actions is due to delusion springing from the quality of *tamas*. The refraining from works because they are painful and from the dread of annoyance ariseth from the quality of *rajas* which belongs to passion, and he who thus leaves undone what he ought to do shall not obtain the fruit which comes from right forsaking. The work which is performed, O Arjuna, because it is necessary, obligatory, and proper, with all self-interest therein put aside and attachment to the action absent, is declared to be of the quality of truth and goodness which is known as *sattva*. The true renouncer, full of the quality of goodness, wise and exempt from all doubt, is averse neither to those works which fail nor those which succeed. It is

67

impossible for mortals to utterly abandon actions; but he who gives up the results of action is the true renouncer. The threefold results of action -- unwished for, wished for, and mixed -- accrue after death to those who do not practice this renunciation, but no results follow those who perfectly renounce.

"Learn, O great-armed one, that for the accomplishment of every work five agents are necessary, as is declared. These are the substratum, the agent, the various sorts of organs, the various and distinct movements and with these, as fifth, the presiding deities. These five agents are included in the performance of every act which a man undertaketh, whether with his body, his speech, or his mind. This being thus, whoever because of the imperfection of his mind beholdeth the real self as the agent thinketh wrongly and seeth not aright. He whose nature is free from egotism and whose power of discrimination is not blinded does not slay though he killeth all these people, and is not bound by the bonds of action. The three causes which incite to action are knowledge, the thing to be known, and the knower, and threefold also is the totality of the action in the act, the instrument, and the agent. Knowledge, the act, and the agent are also distinguished in three ways according to the three qualities; listen to their enumeration after that classification.

"Know that the wisdom which perceives in all nature one single principle, indivisible and incorruptible, not separate in the separate objects seen, is of the *sattva* quality. The knowledge which perceives different and manifold principles as present in the world of created beings pertains to *rajas,* the quality of passion. But that knowledge, wholly without value, which is mean, attached to one object alone as if it were the whole, which does not see the true cause of existence, is of the nature of *tamas,* indifferent and dark.

"The action which is right to be done, performed without attachment to results, free from pride and selfishness, is of the *sattva* quality. That one is of the *rajas* quality which is done with a view to its consequences, or with great exertion, or with egotism. And that which in consequence of delusion is undertaken without regard to its consequences, or the power to carry it out, or the harm it may cause, is of the quality of darkness -- *tamas.*

"The doer who performs necessary actions unattached to their consequences and without love or hatred is of the nature of the quality of truth -- *sattva.* The doer whose actions are performed with attachment to the result, with great exertion, for the gratification of his lusts and with pride, covetousness, uncleanness, and attended with rejoicing and grieving, is of the quality of *rajas* -- passion and desire. The doer who is ignorant, foolish, undertaking actions without ability, without discrimination, with sloth, deceit, obstinacy, mischievousness, and dilatoriness, is of the quality of *tamas*.

"Hear now, O Dhananjaya, conqueror of wealth, the differences which I shall now explain in the discerning power and the steadfast power within, according to the three classes flowing from the divisions of the three qualities. The discerning power that knows how to begin and to renounce, what should and what should not be done, what is to be feared and what not, what holds fast and what sets the soul free, is of the *sattva* quality. That discernment, O son of Pritha, which does not fully know what ought to be done and what not, what should be feared and what not, is of the passion-born *rajas* quality. That discriminating power which is enveloped in obscurity, mistaking wrong for right and all things contrary to their true intent and meaning, is of the dark quality of *tamas*.

"That power of steadfastness holding the man together, which by devotion controls every motion of the mind, the breath, the senses and the organs, partaketh of the *sattva* quality. And that which cherisheth duty, pleasure, and wealth, in him who looketh to the fruits of action is of the quality of *rajas*. But that through which the man of low capacity stays fast in drowsiness, fear, grief, vanity and rashness is from the *tamas* quality, O son of Pritha.

"Now hear what are the three kinds of pleasure wherein happiness comes from habitude and pain is ended. That which in the beginning is as poison and in the end as the waters of life, and which arises from a purified understanding, is declared to be of the *sattva* quality. That arising from the connection of the senses with their objects which in the beginning is sweet as the waters of life but at the end like poison, is of the quality of *rajas*. That pleasure is of the dark *tamas* quality which both in the beginning and the end arising from sleep, idleness, and carelessness, tendeth both in the beginning and the end to stupefy the soul. There is no creature on earth nor among the hosts in heaven who is free from these three qualities which arise from nature.

"The respective duties of the four castes, of Brahmans, Kshatriyas, Vaisyas, and Sudras, are also determined by the qualities which predominate in the disposition of each, O harasser of thy foes. The natural duty of a Brahman compriseth tranquillity, purity, self-mastery, patience, rectitude, learning, spiritual discernment, and belief in the existence of another world. Those of the Kshatriya sprung from his nature are valor, glory, strength, firmness, not to flee from the field of battle, liberality and a lordly character. The natural duties of the Vaisya are to till the land, tend cattle and to buy and sell; and that of the Sudra is to serve, as is his natural disposition.

"Men being contented and devoted to their own proper duties attain perfection; hear now how that perfection is attained by devotion to natural duty.

"If a man maketh offering to the Supreme Being who is the source of the works of all and by whom this universe was spread abroad, he thus obtaineth perfection. The performance of the duties of a man's own particular calling, although devoid of excellence, is better than doing the duty of another, however well performed; and he who fulfills the duties obligated by nature, does not incur sin. A man's own natural duty, even though stained with faults, ought not to be abandoned. For all human acts are involved in faults, as the fire is wrapped in smoke. The highest perfection of freedom from action is attained through renunciation by him who in all works has an unfettered mind and subdued heart.

"Learn from me, in brief, in what manner the man who has reached perfection attains to the Supreme Spirit, which is the end, the aim, and highest condition of spiritual knowledge.

"Imbued with pure discrimination, restraining himself with resolution, having rejected the charms of sound and other objects of the senses, and casting off attachment and dislike; dwelling in secluded places, eating little, with speech, body, and mind controlled, engaging in constant meditation and unwaveringly fixed in dispassion; abandoning egotism, arrogance, violence, vanity, desire, anger, pride, and possession, with calmness ever present, a man is fitted to be the Supreme Being. And having thus attained to the Supreme, he is serene, sorrowing no more, and no more desiring, but alike towards all creatures he attains to supreme devotion to me. By this devotion to me he knoweth fundamentally who and what I am and having thus discovered me he enters into me without any intermediate condition. And even the man who is always engaged in action shall attain by my favor to the eternal and incorruptible imperishable abode, if he put his trust in me alone. With thy heart place all thy works on me, prefer me to all else, exercise mental devotion continually, and think constantly of me. By so doing thou shalt by my divine favor surmount every difficulty which surroundeth thee; but if from pride thou wilt not listen to my words, thou shalt undoubtedly be lost. And if, indulging self-confidence, thou sayest 'I will not fight,' such a determination will prove itself vain, for the principles of thy nature will impel thee to engage. Being bound by all past karma to thy natural duties, thou, O son of Kunti, wilt involuntarily do from necessity that which in thy folly thou wouldst not do. There dwelleth in the heart of every creature, O Arjuna, the Master -- *Isvara* -- who by his magic power causeth all things and creatures to revolve mounted upon the universal wheel of time. Take sanctuary with him alone, O son of Bharata, with all thy soul; by his grace thou shalt obtain supreme happiness, the eternal place.

"Thus have I made known unto thee this knowledge which is a mystery more secret than secrecy itself; ponder it fully in thy mind, act as seemeth best unto thee.

"But further listen to my supreme and most mysterious words which I will now for thy good reveal unto thee because thou art dearly beloved of me. Place thy heart upon me as I have declared myself to be, serve me, offer unto me alone, and bow down before me alone, and thou shalt come to me; I swear it, for thou art dear to me. Forsake every other religion and take refuge alone with me; grieve not, for I shall deliver thee from all transgressions. Thou must never reveal this to one who doth not practice mortification, who is without devotion, who careth not to hear it, nor unto him who despiseth me. He who expoundeth this supreme mystery to my worshipers shall come to me if he performs the highest worship of me; and there shall not be among men anyone who will better serve me than he, and he shall be dearest unto me of all on earth. If anyone shall study these sacred dialogues held between us two, I shall consider that I am worshiped by him with the sacrifice of knowledge; this is my resolve. And even the man who shall listen to it with faith and not reviling shall, being freed from evil, attain to the regions of happiness provided for those whose deeds are righteous.

"Hast thou heard all this, O son of Pritha, with mind one-pointed? Has the delusion of thought which arose from ignorance been removed, O Dhananjaya?"

ARJUNA:

"By thy divine power, O thou who fallest not, my delusion is destroyed, I am collected once more; I am free from doubt, firm, and will act according to thy bidding."

SANJAYA:

Thus have I been an ear-witness of the miraculous astonishing dialogue, never heard before, between Vasudeva and the magnanimous son of Pritha. By the favor of Vydsa I heard this supreme mystery of Yoga -- devotion -- even as revealed from the mouth of Krishna himself who is the supreme Master of devotion. And as I again and again remember, O mighty king, this wonderful sacred dialogue between Krishna and Arjuna, I am delighted again and again. Also, as I recall to my memory the wonderful form of Hari, the Lord, my astonishment is great, O king, and I rejoice again and again. Wherever Krishna, the supreme Master of devotion, and wherever the son of Pritha, the mighty archer, may be, there with certainty are fortune, victory, wealth, and wise action; this is my belief.

Lightning Source UK Ltd.
Milton Keynes UK
UKOW02f1631080316

269821UK00001B/156/P